THE
SR-71
BLACKBIRD
STORY

▲ An in-flight overhead frontal view of a USAF Lockheed SR-71A Blackbird in flight over Beale Air Force Base (AFB), California, on 1 June 1988. The aircraft is generating water vapour condensation vortices. (US National Archives at College Park, Maryland, Still Pictures Branch)

THE

SR-71
BLACKBIRD
STORY

MARK A. CHAMBERS

The
History
Press

First published 2017

The History Press
97 St George's Place, Cheltenham, Gloucestershire, GL0 3QB
www.thehistorypress.co.uk

British Library Cataloguing in Publication Data.
A catalogue record for this book is available from the British Library.

ISBN 978 0 7509 7004 4

Typesetting and origination by The History Press
Printed by Thomson Press, India

Cover illustration. *Front*: A USAF 9th
Strategic Reconnaissance Wing Beale AFB,
California-based SR-71 in flight in 1978 (US
National Archives at College Park, MD,
Still Pictures Branch). *Back Cover*: A USAF
SR-71 banks into a morning sunrise in 1978
(US National Archives at College Park, MD,
Still Pictures Branch).

CONTENTS

Perhaps no other aircraft in aviation history managed to remain such a well-kept secret for as long as the United States' Lockheed SR-71 Blackbird. This cutting-edge aircraft took the art of aerial spying to an unprecedented level and did it all from highly clandestine high-speed spy missions over Communist nations during the late 1960s and '70s for the United States Air Force (USAF) and Central Intelligence Agency (CIA) to advanced sonic boom and hypersonic flight research studies for the National Aeronautics and Space Administration (NASA). This book tells the fascinating story of this truly unique aircraft's design and development as well as its famous and ingenious designer Mr Clarence 'Kelly' Johnson.

Numerous individuals deserve great thanks for providing crucial support for the completion of this book. First and foremost, great thanks go to my loving family – wife Lesa, daughter Caitlyn, and sons Patrick and Ryan – for tolerating my ceaseless words of enthusiasm and providing encouragement and support for this project. Great thanks also go to David Pfeiffer (Civil Records Archivist) and the entire staff of the Textual Reference Branch of the US National Archives and Record Administration (NARA) at College Park, Maryland; and Holly Reed and the entire staff of the Still Pictures Branch of the

US NARA at College Park, Maryland. Finally, great thanks go to Amy Rigg, Commissioning Editor at The History Press, for her unwavering and fantastic encouragement and support in seeing this project through to publication.

➤ NASA Lockheed SR-71B (NASA 831) in flight over the Sierra Nevada mountain chain in California during a 1994 flight research mission. This image happens to be one of the most impressive photos of the National Aeronautics and Space Administration's flight research programmes ever taken. (NASA Dryden Flight Research Center)

In 1912, one of the world's most successful and prosperous aerospace companies, the Lockheed Corporation, was established. The then fledgling aircraft company would eventually become an American giant in aviation history. Lockheed's roots originated from the Aleo Hydro-Aeroplane Company of San Francisco. Its founders were the Loughead brothers, Allan and Malcolm. The company's name was changed to the Loughead Aircraft Manufacturing Company in 1916 and moved to Santa Barbara, California. The company became known for the development of its Model F-1 Flying Boat in 1918. Loughead Aircraft Manufacturing Company, however, lost out in the highly competitive early American aviation market and subsequently shut down. Nonetheless, Allan Loughead, Jack Northrop and Kenneth Jay bounced back, establishing a new aircraft company, renamed the Lockheed Aircraft Company, in Hollywood, California. After developing its famous Vega general aviation transport, Lockheed transferred its blossoming aircraft design and development operation to Burbank, California, where it began to prosper. After experiencing financial difficulties during the Great Depression, the newly named Lockheed Corporation recovered well, developing its popular Electra civil transport series during the 1930s.

Since its inception, Lockheed has always preached the pursuit of 'leading edge', highly innovative aircraft concepts to its brilliant team of engineers and aircraft designers. Perhaps Lockheed's most ingenious and ambitious aircraft designer, Clarence 'Kelly' Johnson, best exemplified this corporate aircraft design philosophy in his approach to designing and developing aircraft. Clarence Leonard 'Kelly' Johnson was born on 27 February 1910 in Ishpeming, Michigan. Johnson was of Swedish descent and by the time he was 13 he earned an award in an aircraft design competition for his first aeroplane design. He graduated from Flint Central High School in 1928 and later attended

▲ Clarence Leonard 'Kelly' Johnson in 1975. (CIA)

Flint Junior College (now Mott Community College) before moving on to the University of Michigan (UM), Ann Arbor. He later earned a Master's of Science (MS) from UM in Aeronautical Engineering. When Johnson graduated from UM, Ann Arbor, with his MS in 1933, he took a tool designer job at the Lockheed Company.

Johnson eventually fell in love with Althea Louise Young, a Lockheed accounting department employee. The couple were married in 1937. Johnson gradually rose in the Lockheed ranks to chief research engineer in 1938.

During the Second World War, Johnson was the designer of the famous P-38 Lightning twin-engine fighter and P-80 Shooting Star, the United States' first operational jet fighter. He also had a hand in the design and development of the PV-1 Ventura patrol bomber. In 1952, Johnson became Lockheed's chief engineer. Johnson ultimately rose to the position of vice president of Research and Development at Lockheed in 1956 and vice president of Advanced Development Projects (ADP) in 1958. During the later 1950s, Johnson gained more fame for his leadership role in the design of the famous high-flying U-2 spyplane. Johnson also gained distinction for his leadership roles in the design of the F-104 Starfighter and, most notably, the ultra-advanced SR-71 Blackbird spyplane.

Unfortunately, Althea Louise Johnson passed away in December 1969. Johnson later married his secretary Maryellen Alberta Meade in 1971. Maryellen became critically ill, however, and passed away on 13 October 1980; she was just 46 years old at the time. Johnson then fell in love with and married Nancy Powers Horrigan in late 1980. Johnson later suffered from a prolonged illness, before sadly passing away at St Joseph Medical Center in Burbank, California, on 21 December 1990. He was 80 years old at the time of his passing.

The spirit of innovation instilled in Lockheed for so many years by Kelly Johnson, however, is still alive today, as evidenced by the company's latest

Did You Know?

The Lockheed P-38 Lightning twin-engine fighter, nicknamed the 'Fork-Tailed Devil' by the Germans, shot down more Japanese aircraft during the Second World War than any other United States Army Air Forces (USAAF) fighter aircraft.

◄ USAAF Colonel Charles H. MacDonald and Al Nelson pose beside MacDonald's P-38J Lightning, nicknamed 'Putt Putt Maru' during the latter portion of the Second World War in the Pacific Theatre. (USAF)

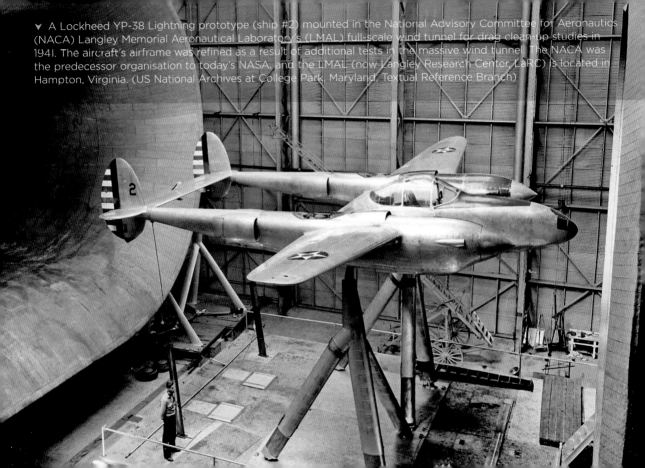

▼ A Lockheed YP-38 Lightning prototype (ship #2) mounted in the National Advisory Committee for Aeronautics (NACA) Langley Memorial Aeronautical Laboratory's (LMAL) full-scale wind tunnel for drag clean-up studies in 1941. The aircraft's airframe was refined as a result of additional tests in the massive wind tunnel. The NACA was the predecessor organisation to today's NASA, and the LMAL (now Langley Research Center, LaRC) is located in Hampton, Virginia. (US National Archives at College Park, Maryland, Textual Reference Branch)

'cutting-edge' military aircraft design achievements: the F-22 Raptor and F-35 Lightning II stealthy, air-superiority fighters. These 'crowning technological achievements' will serve America's national defence needs more strongly than ever before, allowing the nation to proceed more confidently in international affairs well into the new millennium.

Did You Know?

Over 9,000 Lockheed P-38 Lightning fighters were mass-produced during the Second World War.

➤ A Lockheed P-38 Lightning during a weapons demonstration flight at the Army Air Forces Tactical Center in Orlando, Florida. (USAF)

> A Lockheed YP-38 Lightning prototype (ship #2) parked on the tarmac at NACA Langley in 1941. The aircraft awaits wind-tunnel test/flight-test data correlation studies. (NASA Langley Research Center)

Did You Know?

The Lockheed U-2 has served as an all-weather, high-altitude aerial reconnaissance platform for the USAF for more than fifty years.

▲ A USAF Langley-based 27th Fighter Squadron Lockheed Martin F-22A Raptor launches an AIM-120 advanced medium-range air-to-air missile (AMRAAM) during a weapons test over the Gulf of Mexico on 14 February 2006. (USAF/Master Sergeant Michael Ammons)

◄ A Lockheed U-2 spyplane in flight over the coastal waters of Cuba during the early 1960s. (US National Archives at College Park, Maryland, Still Pictures Branch)

Did You Know?

The Lockheed F-104 Starfighter set new world speed and altitude records at the same time in 1958 – the first aeroplane to accomplish this feat in aviation history – and new world altitude/time-to-climb records in 1959.

⌃ A pair of Lockheed F-104As in flight in January 1960. (USAF)

A Lockheed Martin F-35A Lightning II in flight. (US Department of Defense/ USAF Master Sergeant John Nimmo Sr)

The designation 'Skunk Works' was a new term used to refer to the Lockheed Advanced Development Projects. The 'Skunk Works' designation originated from the moonshine factory referred to in *Li'l Abner* comic strips. The Lockheed Skunk Works originated with Lockheed's secret undertaking of the design and development of the XP-80 jet fighter in October 1943. The company completed the jet's design and development in a little over four months. Skunk Works carried this momentum over into its next major project: the design and development of the high-altitude U-2 spyplane, initiated in 1955.

During the early 1960s, Skunk Works commenced design and development efforts on an ultra-advanced, next-generation interceptor/spyplane series: the A-11/A-12/YF-12/SR-71 series. In the decades to follow, Skunk Works went on to produce the highly successful F-117 Nighthawk stealth attack aircraft, as well as today's stealthy F-22 Raptor and F-35 Lightning II air-superiority fighters.

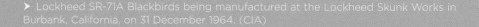

➤ Lockheed SR-71A Blackbirds being manufactured at the Lockheed Skunk Works in Burbank, California, on 31 December 1964. (CIA)

Did You Know?

In 1990, Lockheed transferred its Skunk Works from Burbank, California, to Site 10, USAF Plant 42, Palmdale, California.

Did You Know?

Skunk Works commenced secretive production work on two 'Have Blue' F-117 Nighthawk stealth fighter prototype aircraft, in 1976.

In 1955, the subsonic, high-altitude photo-reconnaissance Lockheed U-2 successfully performed its first test flight. In 1956, the U-2 performed its first operational mission, a secret surveillance overflight of the Soviet Union. Clandestine U-2 spy missions over the Soviet Union continued free of detection by Soviet surface-to-air missile (SAM) site radar systems for four years. Then, on 1 May 1960, a USAF/CIA U-2 piloted by Francis Gary Powers was brought down by a Soviet SAM. Since that disastrous day in 1960, the US has never performed a secret surveillance overflight of the Soviet Union nor the now non-Communist Russia again. Lockheed officials, including Kelly Johnson, sensed the dire need to develop a new, advanced spyplane that was virtually impervious to radar detection and SAMs. Kelly Johnson later recalled this desperate situation in a technical paper he authored entitled 'Development of the Lockheed SR-71 Blackbird' (in *Recollections from the 'Skunk Works'*):

Continuing concern for having a balanced reconnaissance force made it apparent that we still would need a manned reconnaissance aircraft that could be dispatched on worldwide missions when required. From vulnerability studies, we derived certain design requirements for this craft. These were a cruising speed well over

Mach 3, cruising altitude over 80,000 feet, and a very low radar cross-section over a wide band of frequencies. Electronic countermeasures and advanced communications gear were mandatory. The craft should have at least two engines for safety reasons.[1]

Lockheed engineers quickly learned of the tremendous design challenges they faced in developing such an advanced spyplane, which included designing an aircraft capable of flying at ram air temperatures in excess of 800°F. Therefore, it was decided to use heat-resistant titanium and stainless steel for the structural elements of this radical, new aircraft design. Other structural elements of the aircraft, including radomes, had to be made of heat-resistant plastic. The aircraft design

Did You Know?

Blackbirds were given a dark-blue, nearly black, paint finish to enhance internal heat emission and blend in with the darkness of night. Hence, the SR-71 was appropriately nicknamed 'Blackbird'.

also required the use of a special fuel – capable of remaining stable at extremely cold temperatures (less than -90°F) and extremely high temperatures (in excess of 350°F). According to Johnson, 'Cooling the cockpit and crew turned out to be seven times as difficult as on the X-15 research airplane which flew as much as twice as fast as the SR-71 but only for a few minutes per flight.'[2]

In addition, design provisions and accommodations had to be made to protect the landing gear, wheels and tyres from the extreme heat. It was therefore decided to 'bury' these vital landing structures deep within the fuselage fuel tanks. The crew escape system had to be designed such that it afforded the crew the utmost safety when ejecting at a speed of Mach 4 and at an altitude in excess of 100,000ft. Additionally, advanced pilot pressure suits, gear and life-support systems, as well as parachutes, had to be conceived, manufactured and thoroughly tested.

The last advanced spyplane design challenge facing Lockheed engineers was to solve the dilemma of snapping photos through aircraft windows while the aircraft was experiencing extreme heat-affected turbulent airflows along its fuselage.

From April 1958 to September 1959, Johnson strongly proposed the idea of developing a Mach 3 spyplane to CIA official Richard Bissell and the USAF. The new series of proposed spyplanes were to be designated A-1 to A-12. The proposed Lockheed spyplane series design went up against advanced spyplane designs proposed by the General Dynamics Corporation, Convair, and an internal navy design. Ultimately, the Lockheed A-12 design won the contract competition on 29 August 1959. Over the next four months, extensive wind-tunnel tests were conducted, with the green light for actual design, development and flight-testing of twelve aeroplanes being given on 30 January 1960.

The first A-12 spyplane successfully performed its first test flight, with Lockheed test pilot Louis Schalk piloting the aircraft, over the Lockheed flight test facility at Groom Lake (Area 51), Nevada, on 26 April 1962. During its first supersonic flight test conducted on 4 May 1962, the first A-12 attained a speed of Mach 1.1. With newly outfitted Pratt & Whitney J58 engines in early 1963, A-12s attained speeds approaching Mach 3.2. The final A-12 produced arrived at Groom Lake in June 1964. The Lockheed A-12s performed a total of 2,850 test flights. Eighteen Lockheed SR-71 predecessors (thirteen A-12s, three YF-12A USAF interceptors and two M-21 reconnaissance drone carriers) were produced. Three A-12s were lost in crashes, with a fourth loss, in which CIA pilot Walter Ray was killed, taking place at Groom Lake on 5 January 1967.

With the war situation in Vietnam spiralling out of control, A-12s were deployed to Kadena Air Force Base, Okinawa, by order of the CIA Director on 22 May 1967 to perform surveillance missions over North Vietnam as part of Operation Black Shield. Their primary objective was to photograph SAM sites while cruising at a speed of Mach 3.1 at an altitude of 80,000ft. Twenty-two surveillance missions over North Vietnam were flown by A-12s during the Vietnam War. In addition to performing surveillance missions over Vietnam in 1968, Black Shield A-12s performed surveillance overflights of North Korea when the *Pueblo* crisis commenced.

During their secret surveillance overflights of North Vietnam, A-12s became increasingly subjected to the SAM threat, as the North Vietnamese began to acquire more sophisticated Soviet-made SAM defence systems. Throughout 1967, high-flying A-12s were tracked by North Vietnamese SAM radar systems. However, on 28 October 1967, a lone North Vietnamese SAM was launched at an overflying A-12, but it was successfully evaded through the use of A-12 on-board electronic countermeasures systems. The SAM threat became

◄ A Lockheed
M-21/D-21 drone
combo performing
a Project Tagboard
mission in 1966. (CIA)

Did You Know?

On a surveillance flight over North Korea on 26 January 1968, an A-12, piloted by Jack Weeks, captured the location of the North Korean-seized USS *Pueblo* using photographic intelligence.

➤ A Lockheed A-12 in flight during the 1960s. (USAF)

more apparent and nerve-racking, as experienced by A-12 pilot Dennis Sullivan on a mission over North Vietnam on 30 October 1967. During the overflight, a total of six SAMs were launched at his aircraft, with the majority exploding well behind. However, one exploded 100–200yd away from his A-12. When Sullivan returned to his base, it was discovered by ground crews that shrapnel from the close SAM detonation knifed through the lower right-wing fillet section and wedged itself parallel with the wing tank support structure.

The last Black Shield A-12 overflight of North Vietnam was performed on 8 March 1968 and yielded great photos of Khe Sanh and the border regions of Laos, Cambodia and South Vietnam. Three A-12 surveillance overflights of North Korea were also performed in 1968 after the US Navy intelligence ship *Pueblo* was seized by North Korean forces on 23 January. The primary objective of these surveillance overflights was to ascertain if North Korean forces had executed any further belligerent actions and determine the position of the seized *Pueblo*. Aerial-reconnaissance photography, later analysed from the mission, showed that the ship was at anchor in Wonsan Bay under the guard of several North Korean Navy patrol boats. A second surveillance mission over North Korea, in which two overflights were made, was performed on 19 February 1968, which yielded photography of eighty-four high-priority targets and eighty-nine additional targets. The third, and last, A-12 overflight of North Korea was performed by Ronald L. Layton on 8 May 1968.

Perhaps the most intriguing A-12 variant to be produced was the M-21 reconnaissance drone carrier. The Lockheed D-21 was an unmanned high-speed, high-altitude reconnaissance drone that was carried by the M-21 on a dorsal pylon mount. The M-21 was also a two-seat aircraft, accommodating a launch control operator/officer (LCO) in a rear cockpit. The D-21 was supposed to overfly the target then cruise to a rendezvous location, where it

◄ The retired A-12 fleet as stored at Palmdale, California, in 1968. (CIA)

➤ A surviving Lockheed A-12 on static display during Air Force Week in New York City aboard the USS *Intrepid* Sea, Air, and Space Museum on 24 August 2010. (USAF/Lance Cheung)

would eject a mission data article and then explode. The data article was to be snatched in mid-air by a specially equipped C-130 Hercules. Unfortunately, the M-21 programme was terminated in 1966 following an in-air accident in which a D-21 crashed into an M-21 after launch from the M-21. Despite a successful crew ejection, the LCO was lost when his pressure suit collected too much seawater following an ocean splashdown.

While the M-21 was cancelled as a result of this tragic mishap, the D-21B emerged as another viable advanced spy vehicle option when it was successfully carried and launched by B-52 bombers via underwing pylons. The unique spy drone performed admirably during surveillance overflights of China from 1969–71.

On 28 December 1966, it was decided to terminate the A-12 programme due to budgetary problems and a heavier reliance on the new SR-71 Blackbird to fulfil America's clandestine aerial photographic reconnaissance needs. On 21 June 1968, all overseas operational A-12s and eight American mainland-based A-12s were mothballed in a storage facility in Palmdale, California. After almost twenty years in this storage facility, the A-12s were donated to museums throughout the United States. One was even sent to CIA headquarters in Langley, Virginia, where it was put on static display.

On 16–17 March 1960, Lockheed officials, including Kelly Johnson, entered discussions with USAF General Hal Estes in Washington, DC, concerning the design and development of a long-range interceptor version, derived from the Lockheed A-12, of the soon to be developed SR-71 Blackbird, which later became known as the Lockheed YF-12A. After receiving endorsements from both General Estes and USAF Research and Development Secretary Dr Courtlandt Perkins, the Lockheed design team moved up to deliberations with Wright Field General Marvin Demler.

At the time, Lockheed was competing with North America and F-108 interceptor design for the long-range interceptor design and development contract. Lockheed ultimately won the contract, but before they did so, General Demler requested that Lockheed utilise the Hughes ASG-18 radar and AIM-47 Falcon (GAR-9) missiles in the aircraft design, which they later did after rigorously flight testing these operational and weapon systems with Hughes. The first YF-12A successfully performed a test flight on 7 August 1963.

On 24 February 1964, President Lyndon B. Johnson publicly acknowledged the existence of the aircraft in a speech. The YF-12A public existence acknowledgement was really a cover for the clandestine

A-12 programme. A total of three YF-12As were produced and based at Edwards AFB, California. Although an order for ninety-three F-12B production variants was requested by the USAF Air Defense Command (ADC) on 14 May 1965, Secretary of Defense Robert McNamara refused to fund its development as a result of skyrocketing Vietnam War expenses, and the threat to the US homeland was considered at the time to not be great. Consequently, the F-12B programme was terminated in January 1968.

In USAF YF-12A flight tests, the three test aircraft established a new speed record of 2,070.101mph and a new altitude record of 80,257.86ft, both of which were set on 1 May

1965. In addition, a total of six successful AIM-47 air-to-air missile launches were conducted. The final AIM-47 missile firing was performed while the aircraft was cruising at a speed of Mach 3.2 and an altitude of 74,000ft, destroying a ground-launched JQB-47E target drone

⌃ The first Lockheed YF-12A interceptor successfully performs its first flight in the skies above Edwards AFB, California, on 7 August 1963. (US National Archives at College Park, Maryland, Still Pictures Branch)

⌃ The roll out of the first Lockheed YF-12A interceptor at Edwards AFB, California, for its first flight on 7 August 1963. Later, on 29 February 1964, President Lyndon B. Johnson revealed its existence to the public in a speech, which was a cover for the existence of the Lockheed A-12, already being flight tested at Area 51 in the Nevada desert. (US National Archives at College Park, Maryland, Still Pictures Branch)

that was cruising at an altitude of only 500ft. USAF YF-12A test pilot Jim Irwin later became an Apollo programme astronaut with NASA and gained fame when he successfully performed an extra-vehicular activity (EVA) or walk on the lunar surface during Apollo 15 in midsummer 1971.

After F-12B production plans were scrapped, the YF-12A programme was terminated. However, USAF YF-12As were still flown on occasion by the air force and NASA in flight research missions. Air force YF-12As performed B-1 bomber flight-simulation studies and flight experimentation regarding the YF-12A's performance in a tactical setting, as well as evaluating

Did You Know?

On 1 May 1965, YF-12A (60-6936), piloted by Colonel Robert L. 'Fox' Stephens with Lieutenant Colonel Daniel Andre serving as fire control officer (FCO), set an altitude record of 80,257.86ft during a test flight.

◄ A USAF Lockheed YF-12A on a test flight above Edwards AFB in 1964. (US National Archives at College Park, Maryland, Still Pictures Branch)

> Lockheed aircraft designer Kelly Johnson and his brainchild, the YF-12A, at Edwards AFB, California on 15 July 1965. (US National Archives at College Park, Maryland, Still Pictures Branch)

its suitability for coordinated operations with airborne early warning and control (AEW&C) aircraft. NASA YF-12A flight research studies, conducted from December 1969 to November 1979, focused on determining the effects of inlet performance on airframe and engine thrust interaction, studying boundary layer noise, aerothermodynamics at high speeds and supersonic high-altitude cruise flight characteristics.

To complete another interesting NASA flight research study, the space agency acquired a YF-12C specially modified to accommodate and launch a NASA HT-4 drone, capable of flying at hypersonic speeds (speeds in excess of

◄ A NASA Lockheed YF-12A on a test flight above NASA Dryden Flight Research Center at Edwards AFB, California. (NASA Dryden Flight Research Center)

Mach 5), while flying at the YF-12C's cruise altitude and maximum Mach number. The drone was outfitted with a Pratt & Whitney RL-10 liquid-rocket engine. NASA thoroughly studied a multitude of mounting configurations as well as its operational feasibilies. Initially, flyaway and impulse launching methods were reviewed, but later it was finally decided that the aerodynamic lift-launch method was best for ensuring safe and effective drone separation from the YF-12C mothership. Prior to launch, a special launch beam was elevated to a vertical orientation, which helped to elevate the drone and facilitate positive lift. The NASA YF-12C/Hypersonic HT-4 Drone flight research study proved to be highly successful and revealed that the aerodynamic lift launch method for such research purposes could consistently achieve mission success.

Only one YF-12A (AF Serial No. 60-06935) exists today, and it is proudly displayed at the National Museum of the United States Air

>> The underside of a USAF Lockheed YF-12A on a test flight above Edwards AFB on 30 September 1964. (US National Archives at College Park, Maryland, Still Pictures Branch)

◁ A USAF YF-12A on a test flight above Edwards AFB on 30 September 1964, with a USAF Flight Test Center F-104 Starfighter flying chase. (US National Archives at College Park, Maryland, Still Pictures Branch)

>> A USAF Lockheed YF-12A makes a return taxi to its Edwards AFB hangar following a test flight in which the aircraft's capabilities were demonstrated to the public on 30 September 1964. (US National Archives at College Park, Maryland, Still Pictures Branch)

>> USAF and NASA crews pose for a publicity photo in front of a USAF YF-12A at rest on the ramp at the Air Force Flight Test Center (AFFTC) at Edwards AFB, California, on 29 June 1970. (US National Archives at College Park, Maryland, Still Pictures Branch)

Force at Wright-Patterson AFB close to Dayton, Ohio.

Did You Know?

During the test flight performed on 1 May 1965, the same YF-12A, crewed by the same airmen, set a speed record, flown over a straight course, of 2,070.101mph.

⌃ A USAF Lockheed YF-12A parked on the ramp at the AFFTC at Edwards AFB, California, on 29 June 1970. (US National Archives at College Park, Maryland, Still Pictures Branch)

⌃ Head-on view of a USAF YF-12A at the AFFTC at Edwards AFB, California, on 30 September 1964. (US National Archives at College Park, Maryland, Still Pictures Branch)

The birth of the SR-71 and the USAF-Pentagon endorsement of its concept signalled exciting times ahead for Lockheed. The mood and state of affairs at the time was best described later by Kelly Johnson:

In early January 1961, I made the first proposal for a strategic reconnaissance bomber to Dr Joseph Charyk, Secretary of the Air Force, Colonel Leo Geary, our Pentagon project officer on the YF-12; and Mr Lew Meyer, a high financial officer in the Air Force. We were encouraged to continue our company-funded studies on the aircraft. As we progressed in the development, we encountered very strong opposition in certain Air Force quarters on the part of those trying to save the North American B-70 programme, which was in considerable trouble. Life became very interesting in that we were competing the SR-71 with an airplane five times its weight and size. On 4 June 1962 the Air Force evaluation team reviewed our design and the mock-up – and we were given good grades.

Our discussions continued with the Department of Defense and also, in this period, with General Curtis LeMay and his Strategic Air Command officers. It was on 27 December 1962 that we were finally put on contract to build the first group of six SR-71 aircraft.

Did You Know?

The Blackbird's airframe, specifically its fuselage panels, expands by numerous inches during high-speed flight due to excessive heat and, therefore, are joined loosely during pre-high-speed flight. The aircraft's inboard wing skins consist of corrugated aluminium to facilitate vertical and horizontal expansion, which also acts to enhance the structural strength of the aircraft.

◀ The aerodynamically sleek features of the Blackbird are shown to effect in this frontal view of the first SR-71A in its hangar at Edwards AFB, California, on 11 May 1965. (US National Archives at College Park, Maryland, Still Pictures Branch)

> The instrument panel in the pilot's cockpit of a SR-71 Blackbird. (US National Archives at College Park, Maryland, Still Pictures Branch)

One of our major problems during the next few years was in adapting our Skunk Works operating methods to provide SAC with proper support, training, spare parts, and data required for their special operational needs. I have always believed that our Strategic Air Command is one of the most sophisticated and demanding customers for aircraft in the world. The fact that we have been able to support them so well for many years is one of the most satisfying aspects of my career.

Without the total support of such people as General Leo Geary in the Pentagon and a long series of extremely competent and helpful commanding officers at Beale

Air Force Base, we could never have jointly put the Blackbirds into service successfully.[3]

In designing the SR-71, the Lockheed team determined that a thin delta-wing platform configuration was best suited for the aircraft design and its unique clandestine mission. Lockheed engineers decided to build around a long, slender fuselage that could hold large amounts of fuel and accommodate the landing gear and payloads. The aircraft's fuselage possessed lateral chine surfaces, strategically positioned along the fuselage to mitigate the aerodynamic performance hindering effects of wing-trim drag. The chines also transformed the forward portion of the aircraft into a sort of fixed canard that facilitated lift. The SR-71's skin was made of advanced radar-absorbing materials. The aircraft also made use of cesium fuel additives to mitigate exhaust plume detection by enemy radar. According to Johnson:

The hardest design problem on the airplane was making the engine air inlet and ejector work properly. The inlet cone moves almost three feet to keep the shock wave where we want it. A hydraulic actuator, computer controlled, has to provide operating forces of up to 31,000 pounds under certain flow conditions in the nacelles. To account for the effect of the fuselage chine air flow, the inlets

▲ The roll-out of the trainer variant of the Blackbird, the SR-71B, in 1965. The SR-71B became operational with the 4200th Strategic Reconnaissance Wing at Beale AFB, California, in late 1965. (US National Archives at College Park, Maryland, Still Pictures Branch)

are pointed down and in toward the fuselage.[4]

Wind-tunnel testing through all speed regimes was conducted on the A-12, YF-12A and SR-71 aircraft designs. In addition, full-scale fuel-feed tests were performed, using a special test set-up, at a multitude of simulated altitudes. The most extensive wind-tunnel tests were aimed at enhancing the nacelle inlets, bleed designs and ejector. The SR-71 propulsion system development proved to be quite unique. As stated by Kelly Johnson:

We learned that it often required over 600 horsepower to get the Pratt & Whitney J-58 engine up to starting RPM. To obtain this power, we took two Buick racing car engines and developed a gear box to connect them both to the J-58 starter drive. We operated for several years with this setup, until more sophisticated air starting systems were developed and installed in the hangars.[5]

In building the first Blackbird, several structural factors had to be considered. According to Kelly Johnson, these included:

1. Only titanium and steel had the ability to withstand the operating temperatures encountered.
2. Aged B-120 titanium weighs one half as much as stainless steel per

cubic inch but its ultimate strength is almost up to stainless.

3. Conventional construction could be used with fewer parts involved than with steel.

4. High strength composites were not available in the early 1960s. We did develop a good plastic which has been remarkably serviceable but it was not used for primary structure.[6]

When it came to manufacturing the space-age new materials to be used on the Blackbird, Lockheed's approach was truly unique. As stated by Kelly Johnson:

We developed a complex quality control programme. For every batch of ten parts or more we processed three test coupons which were subjected to the identical heat treatment of the parts in the batch. One coupon was tensile tested to failure to derive the stress-strain data. A quarter-of-an-inch cut was made in the edge of the second coupon by a sharp scissor-like cutter and it was then bent around a mandrel at the cut. If the coupon could not be bent 180°

▼ The first USAF SR-71A in 1966. (US National Archives at College Park, Maryland, Still Pictures Branch)

at a radius of X times the sheet thickness without breaking, it was considered to be too brittle. (The value of X is a function of the alloy used and the stress/strain value of the piece .) The third coupon was held in reserve if any reprocessing was required.[7]

* * *

Drilling and machining high strength titanium alloys, such as B-120, required a complete research programme to determine best tool cutter designs, cutting fluids, and speeds and feeds for best metal removal rates. We had particular trouble with wing extrusions which were used by the thousands of feet. Initially, the cost of machining a foot out of the rolled mill part was $19.00 which was reduced to $11.00 after much research. At one time we were approaching the ability at our vendor's plants to roll parts to net dimensions, but the final achievement of this required a $30,000,000 new facility which was not built.

* * *

Our overall research on titanium usage was summarized in reports which we furnished not only to the Air Force but also to our vendors who machined over half of our machined parts for the programme. To use titanium efficiently required an on-going training programme for thousands of

people – both ours in manufacturing and in the Air Force in service.

Throughout this and other programmes, it has been crystal clear to me that our country needs a $250,000-ton metal forging press – five times as large as our biggest one available today. When we have to machine away 90 percent of our rough forgings today both in titanium (SR-71 nacelle rings and landing gears) and aluminium (C-5 fuselage side rings) it seems that we are nationally very stupid! My best and continuing efforts to solve this problem have been defeated for many years. Incidentally, the USSR has been much smarter in this field in that it has more and larger forging presses than we do.[8]

Did You Know?

In 1964, Kelly Johnson was awarded his second Collier Trophy, one of aviation's highest awards, for his role in the design and development of the SR-71 Blackbird. Johnson was awarded his first Collier Trophy in 1959 for his role in the design and development of the supersonic F-104 Starfighter interceptor.

◀◀ The first USAF SR-71A in flight in 1966. (US National Archives at College Park, Maryland, Still Pictures Branch)

Did You Know?

The Blackbird performed a nonstop flight from New York to London in one hour fifty-five minutes and subsequently performed a nonstop return flight from London to Beale AFB, California, in three hours forty-eight minutes. Now that's fast!

The first SR-71 Blackbird performed the inaugural test flight on 23 December 1964 at Air Force Plant 42 in Palmdale, California. During further flight tests of the new Blackbird, a maximum speed of Mach 3.4 was attained. Blackbirds became operational, flying for the 4200th (eventually, 9th) Strategic Reconnaissance Wing, at Beale AFB, California, in January 1966. Thirty-two Blackbirds were ultimately produced, with a total of twelve being written off in crashes caused by technical operational problems.

◄ A USAF 9th Strategic Reconnaissance Wing SR-71A lands at the Farnborough Air Show, England, after setting a new transatlantic speed record on 1 September 1974. (US National Archives at College Park, Maryland, Still Pictures Branch)

Artistic rendition by artist Hal McCormick, entitled 'SR-71: First Operational Mission', depicting an SR-71 on its first operational mission. (US National Archives at College Park, Maryland, Still Pictures Branch)

The SR-71 had entered operational service with the USAF just in time to be deployed for secretive high-speed, high-flying aerial photo-reconnaissance missions over North Vietnam during the Vietnam War. On 8 March 1968, the first batch of SR-71s was deployed, as part of the 9th SRW, at Operating Location (OL-8) at Kadena AFB, Okinawa. Their operational deployments during the Vietnam War became known as 'Glowing Heat'. This clandestine programme became known as 'Senior Crown'. The actual overflights of North Vietnam became known as 'Giant Scale'. The first Blackbird overflight of North Vietnam was performed by SR-71 serial no. 61-7976, piloted by Major Jerome F. O'Malley and Captain Edward D. Payne, on 21 March 1968. The mission was launched from Kadena AFB, Okinawa. Major O'Malley later rose to the rank of general.

During the mission, Major O'Malley and Captain Payne used cameras and a Goodyear side-looking airborne radar (SLAR) in the aircraft's nose to take high-quality photos of key strategic enemy positions and forces. The photos taken by the Blackbird showed the positions of numerous artillery batteries near Khe Sanh as well as support vehicles. Consequently, American air raids were launched for the next several days to take these targets out, which helped to bring an end to the seventy-seven-day siege being endured by US forces there. O'Malley and Payne later received the Distinguished Flying Cross for their actions during this mission. SR-71 serial no. 61-7976 went on to successfully perform 942 missions, the most among all Blackbirds. These missions were flown from Beale AFB; Palmdale, California; Kadena AFB, Okinawa, Japan; and RAF Mildenhall, UK. This aeroplane is presently on static display at the National Museum of the United States Air Force close to Dayton, Ohio.

Initially, SR-71s performed overflights of North Vietnam, Laos and Cambodia in 1968. At this time, the aircraft flew primarily only one mission per week. This

◀ An SR-71A crew board their Blackbird prior to taking off on a mission from Beale AFB, California, in 1969. (US National Archives at College Park, Maryland, Still Pictures Branch)

continued for almost two years. Then, in 1970, Blackbirds flew an average of two missions per week. By 1972, Blackbirds flew one mission daily. Unfortunately, two Blackbirds crashed during the Vietnam War, both resulting from technical problems with on-board aircraft operational systems. Hundreds of SAMs were launched as Blackbirds during the war, but none ever struck their targets – a testament to the SR-71's great speed and radar-evading capabilities. During a tour of duty in Okinawa, the Okinawans began to call the Blackbirds and their aircrews 'Habu'. This term is used to refer to a Japanese pit viper. In response, Blackbird crews at Kadena AFB adorned their aircraft with Habu squadron markings as well as small Habu successful mission completion markings.

Equipped with new Loral high-resolution radar (HRR), SR-71s were used to photographically survey lines of communication and supply between ports in North Vietnam and North Vietnam's borders with China in June 1972. In addition to using HRR, the Blackbirds used electromagnetic reconnaissance (EMR) equipment to gather electronic intelligence (ELINT). The only night mission to be carried out by the Blackbird during the Vietnam War occurred just prior to midnight on 27 December 1972. The mission was performed by SR-71 975 and piloted by Colonel Darrell Cobb, with Captain Reggie Blackwell serving as reconnaissance systems officer RSO, flying from Kadena AFB. The aircraft performed a coordinated EMR-HRR mission aimed at revealing whether or not North Vietnam had obtained advanced SAM systems or hardware from the Soviets or enhanced SA-2 operations, which could have accounted for numerous B-52s previously being shot down.

▸▸ The same SR-71A as previously pictured taking off from Beale AFB, California, in 1969. (US National Archives at College Park, Maryland, Still Pictures Branch)

Did You Know?

During the Vietnam War, USAF 9th SRW Blackbirds successfully performed a total of sixty-seven overflights of North Vietnam in 1968 alone.

◄ The famous Blackbird 'Ichi Ban', an SR-71A, in flight in 1972. This aircraft flew many missions during the Vietnam War, which were denoted as individual 'Habu' (Japanese pit viper) markings behind the RSO's cockpit on the fuselage port side of the aircraft. (US National Archives at College Park, Maryland, Still Pictures Branch)

⌃ An SR-71B taxies past the control tower at Beale AFB, California, on 13 March 1970. (US National Archives at College Park, Maryland, Still Pictures Branch)

⌃ Front view of an SR-71A in 1974. (US National Archives at College Park, Maryland, Still Pictures Branch)

The SR-71 overflight was conducted simultaneously with a force of sixty B-52s bombing the Lang Dang, Duc Noi and Trung Quant rail yards, as well as the Van Dien supply depot and a trio of SAM sites. The intent was to overwhelm North Vietnamese radar defences while the SR-71 snuck into the North Vietnamese airspace undetected. Using its advanced ECM systems, the Blackbird also lent a SAM system jamming hand to the massive B-52 bombers. The mission proved to be a

> An SR-71A crew pose for a publicity photo in front of their revolutionary aircraft upon the Blackbird's first operational stint at Beale AFB, California. (US National Archives at College Park, Maryland, Still Pictures Branch)

An SR-71A in flight above Beale AFB, California, in 1969. (US National Archives at College Park, Maryland, Still Pictures Branch)

great success. As a result of SR-71 975's impressive ECM shield emitted during the mission, only two B-52s were lost. In addition, the Blackbird's ELINT data showed the locations of two emitters that heavily contributed to B-52 shoot-downs. Consequently, two additional 60-B-52 Linebacker II bombing missions, conducted on the last two nights of the bombing offensive (Linebacker II), concluded effectively and without a single B-52 loss. With the help of the SR-71 Blackbird, the Linebacker II bombing offensive helped to bring the North Vietnamese back to the negotiating table and to sign the Peace Accord in Paris on 27 January 1973, which effectively brought the Vietnam War, for the United States, to an end.

Did You Know?

No Blackbirds were lost to fire from enemy forces during the conflict in Vietnam.

▲ Side view of the famous Blackbird 'Ichi Ban' in flight above Beale AFB, California, in 1972. (US National Archives at College Park, Maryland, Still Pictures Branch)

‹ A USAF SR-71A taxies in front of a line-up of KC-135 tankers and a Strategic Air Command B-52 at Beale AFB, California, in 1972. (US National Archives at College Park, Maryland, Still Pictures Branch)

‹ A USAF SR-71B takes off on a dusk training mission on 13 August 1972. (US National Archives at College Park, Maryland, Still Pictures Branch)

On 6 October 1973 (the Jewish 'Day of Atonement' known as Yom Kippur) Israel fell victim to Egyptian and Syrian air and artillery raids. Syria also invaded northern Israel and Egypt invaded the Sinai. Israel suddenly found itself at war with both Egypt and Syria. Israel's ally, the United States, sought to monitor the situation closely and decided to utilise its most advanced, manned aerial recon asset at the time – the Lockheed SR-71 Blackbird. US intelligence officials reasoned that the Blackbird could provide the least crew-risky option and best photographic intelligence (PHOTINT) and ELINT surveillance of the progress of the war. SR-71s flying recon missions over the war zone were originally intended to take off from Beale AFB, California, perform overflights of the battlefield and complete their missions by landing at RAF Mildenhall, England.

However, the British government refused to support the United States' proposed SR-71 overflights, forcing the US to alter the suggested Blackbird flight routes. The SR-71s now had to fly their Yom Kippur war zone surveillance overflights, launching from Griffiss AFB, New York. A batch of Blackbirds were deployed to Griffiss from Beale AFB, California. The first SR-71 (979), flown by Lieutenant Colonel Jim Shelton and Major Gary Coleman and intended for use in the Yom Kippur conflict, arrived at Griffiss AFB on

11 October 1973. SR-71 964 arrived soon thereafter. Unfortunately, this aircraft experienced technical difficulties with its hydraulic systems and required an engine swap – the new engine had to be airlifted to Griffiss from Beale. A KC-135 tanker was deployed from RAF Mildenhall to support the two Blackbirds' aerial refuelling needs. SR-71 979 was about to embark on the longest Blackbird mission yet.

At 02.00 on 11 October 1973, SR-71 979 took off from Griffiss, headed for the Middle East, on the first surveillance mission of the Yom Kippur war zone. A total of nine Giant Reach/Busy Pilot sorties were flown. The aircraft was the recipient of a total of six aerial refuellings. Once the Blackbird approached the war zone, a combat air patrol (CAP), consisting of US Navy carrier-borne fighters or fleet defenders, flew cover for the inbound Blackbird. The aircraft performed an overflight of Port Said before loitering for twenty-five minutes in prohibited airspace above the battlefield. The Blackbird surveyed the Israeli, Egyptian and Syrian battlegrounds before performing three more aerial refuelings with tankers and completing the long leg back to Griffiss. The mission lasted a total of ten hours eighteen minutes, with half of the mission being flown at speeds in excess of Mach 3. As a result of this precedent-setting mission, the US provided its ally, Israel, with invaluable

>> A USAF SR-71A taking off from Beale AFB, California, in 1972. (US National Archives at College Park, Maryland, Still Pictures Branch)

intelligence regarding Arab positions as well as their use of Soviet-supplied weapons systems and vehicles.

Did You Know?

During the Blackbird's first combat operational mission of the Yom Kippur War on 11 October 1973, the aircraft stayed aloft for ten hours eighteen minutes, five hours of which was spent at speeds in excess of Mach 3.

On 25 October 1973, Blackbird 979 performed another overflight of the battlefield. American intelligence experts feared that the Soviets might have been providing advisors and advanced weaponry or hardware to Egypt and Syria. Consequently, Blackbird 979's second mission over the war zone involved surveying the Latakia and Tartus shipping ports in Syria and the Egyptian shipping ports of Port Said and Alexandria. The same Blackbird performed a third recon sortie eight days after completing its second. The third mission once again involved surveying the ports but also entailed obtaining detailed photos of Cairo International Airport and the cave complex at Tura. US intelligence

experts also feared that these facilities might have been housing or concealing Soviet-supplied Scud-B mobile missile-launch systems.

On 11 November 1973, Blackbird 964, flown by Majors Jim Wilson and Bruce Douglas, performed its first Yom Kippur recon sortie – taking off from Griffiss on a ten-hour and forty-five-minute mission and returning to the US mainland at Seymour Johnson AFB, North Carolina. Even after a ceasefire was officially negotiated by the United Nations, on 24 October 1973, skirmishes between the opposing forces persisted and once again the two Blackbirds were required to monitor the eventual end of hostilities and withdrawal of belligerent forces. Five additional SR-71 Yom Kippur aftermath recon missions were launched from Seymour Johnson. With the assistance of numerous aerial refuelling efforts by dedicated and reliable KC-135 tankers and their aircrews, the Yom Kippur SR-71 overflights truly and effectively demonstrated the global reach of the Blackbird.

With the premature retirement of the A-12, SR-71s resumed surveillance flights of North Korea as part of the Senior Crown programme. The Blackbird missions were launched from Kadena AFB, Okinawa, Japan. Their recon sortie objectives were achieved through flights over North Korea's coast and the demilitarised zone (DMZ). US intelligence and CIA experts estimated that North Korea's army had dramatically increased in number and strength from 1977 to 1978. In addition, much sabre-rattling had been perpetrated by North Korea's volatile Communist dictator, Kim Il-sung, who also sought to make Korea a unified country again, but under harsh Communist rule. America's military brass requested that SR-71 recon missions over North Korea be upped from eight to twelve each month. In addition to being outfitted with special cameras to complete two missions as well as the last ten missions, Blackbirds were to make use of their HRR and ELINT systems to collect radar Intelligence.

As a result of North Korea's great capability to mobilise and strengthen its forces during the night, America's military brass also requested that the Blackbird missions be performed during the night. On the night of 19 September 1977, SR-71 960, with pilot Jack Veth and RSO Bill Keller on board, took off from Kadena on the first night-time Blackbird overflight

Did You Know?

On the night of 26 August 1981, SR-71 976, with Major Maury Rosenberg serving as pilot and Captain E.D. McKim serving as RSO, completed a three-time overflight of the DMZ mission after successfully evading a North Korean SA-2 missile.

of North Korea, successfully performing their important surveillance mission before landing at Kadena. The time required to complete the mission was four hours six minutes. However, during these night missions, Blackbird crews found that there were serious flaws in the Blackbird's cockpit lighting systems that required modification. As a result, in 1982, all Blackbirds were equipped with peripheral vision horizon display (PVHD) systems, as well as enhanced cockpit lighting.

Later in April 1981, U2Rs and SR-71s collaborated in joint recon missions over North Korea, providing critical ELINT and intelligence data regarding the development of a SA-2 site on Choc Tarrie

▾ A USAF 1st Strategic Reconnaissance Squadron (SRS) SR-71A taxiing out on a mission while a 349th SRW U-2R (background) lands at Beale AFB, California, on 10 March 1977. (US National Archives at College Park, Maryland, Still Pictures Branch)

Island. These collaborative missions continued well into August. On the night of 25 August, SR-71 967, piloted by Major Nevin Cunningham with Major Geno Quist serving as RSO took off from Kadena on a DMZ two-pass HRR and ELINT surveillance mission. The mission was successfully completed.

The following night, a Blackbird three overflight of the DMZ mission was launched from Kadena, with Major Maury Rosenberg serving as pilot and Captain E.D. McKim serving as RSO aboard SR-71 976. During their third overflight, the Blackbird 976 crew detected an SA-2 launch. The Blackbird's crew lit the aircraft's afterburners and opened the throttle so that the aircraft reached an airspeed of Mach 3.2, easily outrunning the missile, which exploded 2 miles from the aircraft.

On 26 October 1981, SR-71 975, crewed by pilot B.C. Thomas and RSO Jay Reid, launched from Kadena on a sortie similar to the one previously performed by SR-71 976. On this mission, however, Blackbird 975 was supported by USAF 'Wild Weasel' SAM site-destroyer aircraft which was already in the air in the vicinity of the recon area. This action was signed off by President Ronald Reagan. However, the Blackbird mission proceeded as originally planned and was successfully completed in four hours and twelve minutes without incident.

During the late 1970s, America's nemesis to the south, the Soviet satellite nation of Cuba, began to increase tensions with its northern neighbour. Consequently, Blackbirds serving with the 9th SRW were called upon to perform surveillance overflights of Cuba as part of the Senior Crown programme. These missions were launched from Beale AFB, California, and were first code-named Giant Plate. The code name was later changed to Clipper. The majority of the missions were performed in international airspace near the island. The Cuban surveillance missions usually lasted three hours and thirty minutes. Sometimes during the missions, however, Blackbirds actually flew over the island. In 1978, US spy satellite imagery indicated that a Russian freighter had docked in Havana with huge crates on board. It was also discovered that the crates were being transported to an airfield close to the port and that crews were

Did You Know?

In November 1978, Blackbird overflights of Cuba confirmed that the nation had received fifteen MiG-23 Flogger interceptors shipped from the Soviet Union.

▲ A USAF SR-71A Blackbird in banked flight above Beale AFB, California, in 1978. Note the vast KC-135 tanker fleet on the ground below. (US National Archives at College Park, Maryland, Still Pictures Branch)

reassembling aircraft, including fifteen MiG-23 Flogger interceptors destined for operational service with the Cuban Air Force. Before two SR-71 overflights of Cuba were performed in November 1978, US intelligence experts feared that the Floggers could have nuclear weapon-carrying capability, posing a serious threat to the United States. The Blackbird overflights, however, confirmed that the Floggers were purely interceptor variants.

In response to a raid by Libyan terrorists on a packed club in West Berlin in 1986, United States President Ronald Reagan launched Operation Eldorado Canyon on 15 April 1986. The military operation entailed a coordinated attack on various targets within Libya. The attacks were carried out by US Navy carrier-based A-6 Intruder bombers, A-7 Corsair II strike aircraft, F/A-18 Hornet fighter/bombers and RAF Lakenheath-based USAF F-111 Aardvark swing-wing fighter-bombers. To obtain post-attack PHOTINT, SR-71 980 (call sign TROMP 30), operating from RAF Mildenhall, was called upon for duty. The mission would not be easy, however, as it required a daylight overflight of the already attacked target areas and exposure to alerted Libyan SAM defence systems. To ensure mission success, SR-71 980 was backed up by SR-71 960 (TROMP 31), which took off from RAF Mildenhall one hour fifteen minutes after SR-71 980's departure. It turned out that TROMP 30 required no backup.

The mission proved to be a great success, with both Blackbirds safely returning to Mildenhall. SR-71 980's technical objective cameras (TEOCs) and nose optical bar cameras (OBC) functioned flawlessly. A couple of additional Blackbird overflights of Libya were performed on 16 and 17 April. During the Eldorado Canyon

▲ A Det. 4,
9th Strategic
Reconnaissance
Wing, 3rd Air Force
SR-71A Blackbird
taxis out onto the
runway to RAF
Mildenhall. (US
National Archives
at College Park,
Maryland, Still
Pictures Branch)

missions, two SR-71s were in the air simultaneously for the first time. In addition, the missions were the first to utilise KC-10s for Blackbird aerial refuelling in the skies over Europe. Blackbird PHOTINT was also shared with the media for the first time.

Did You Know?

On 15 April 1986, the Blackbird performed overflights of Libya to obtain post-attack PHOTINT of intended targets struck during Operation Eldorado Canyon. Although numerous SAM launches were detected by the Blackbird, none came close to hitting their intended target.

The previously depicted Blackbird is prepped for a mission at RAF Mildenhall. (US National Archives at College Park, Maryland, Still Pictures Branch)

➤ A USAF 9th SRW RAF Mildenhall-based SR-71A in flight. (US National Archives at College Park, Maryland, Still Pictures Branch)

▼ The previously depicted Blackbird lifts off, engines full throttle, from RAF Mildenhall. (US National Archives at College Park, Maryland, Still Pictures Branch)

From the early 1970s to the 1990s, SR-71 Blackbirds tallied an impressive list of remarkable aviation firsts and achievements. In 1974, the Blackbird's veil of secrecy was lifted when the aircraft arrived at Farnborough, England, for its initial public appearance at an international air show, in record-setting fashion. On 1 September 1974, a 9th Strategic Reconnaissance Blackbird established a new transatlantic speed record of one hour fifty-five minutes from New York to London. The same Blackbird followed up this feat by setting another speed record of three hours forty-seven minutes from London to Los Angeles. On 27–28 July 1976, two Strategic Air Command SR-71A Blackbirds broke six world altitude and speed records, including attaining an altitude of 85,068ft and a speed of 2,092mph.

In July 1979 at Beale AFB, California-based 1st Strategic Reconnaissance Squadron SR-71s took part in Global Shield 79 – a broad-scale world-wide Strategic Air Command exercise that was the largest of its kind conducted in twenty years. Another impressive milestone was achieved on 15 January 1982 when SR-71B, air force service no. 61-7956, flew its 1,000th mission. On 22 November 1989, all USAF SR-71 assets were ordered to stand down and the illustrious Blackbird programme officially ended. By 1990, the complete Blackbird fleet, including

A USAF Blackbird completes its mission by making a drag-chute-deployed landing in 1974. (US National Archives at College Park, Maryland, Still Pictures Branch)

its predecessor A-12 and YF-12 fleets, racked up a total of 3,551 successful missions performed, as well as a total of 2,752 hours flown at a speed of Mach 3 during missions.[9]

On the way to its final resting place – permanent static display at the Smithsonian Institution's Steven F. Udvar-Hazy Center in Chantilly, Virginia – and completion of the final Senior Crown mission on 6 March 1990, the last Senior Crown Blackbird shattered four existing speed records.

⌄ A USAF SR-71A on a mission in 1974. (US National Archives at College Park, Maryland, Still Pictures Branch)

Did You Know?

The SR-71 flew at speeds 40 per cent faster than the Concorde commercial supersonic transport.

Did You Know?

On 1 September 1974, a 9th Strategic Reconnaissance Blackbird established a new transatlantic speed record of one hour fifty-five minutes from New York to London. The same Blackbird followed up this feat by setting another speed record of three hours forty-seven minutes from London to Los Angeles.

◄◄ A USAF 9th Strategic Reconnaissance Wing SR-71A on static display at Farnborough Air Show, England, in September 1974. The 1974 air show marked the first time that a Blackbird was statically displayed to the public. (US National Archives at College Park, Maryland, Still Pictures Branch)

◄ Side view of the record-setting Blackbird on the flight line at Farnborough, England, in September 1974. The aircraft's journey originated at Beale AFB, California. (US National Archives at College Park, Maryland, Still Pictures Branch)

▲ A USAF SR-71A lands during an air show at Andrews AFB, Maryland, in July 1976. (US National Archives at College Park, Maryland, Still Pictures Branch)

▶ A USAF SR-71A embarks on a strategic training mission launched from Ellsworth AFB, South Dakota, in July 1975. (US National Archives at College Park, Maryland, Still Pictures Branch)

◀ A USAF SR-71A takes to the skies above Andrews AFB, Maryland, landing gear up, during an air show in July 1976. (US National Archives at College Park, Maryland, Still Pictures Branch)

‹ A USAF SR-71A in flight in 1976. (US National Archives at College Park, Maryland, Still Pictures Branch)

Did You Know?

On 27–28 July 1976, two Strategic Air Command SR-71A Blackbirds broke six world altitude and speed records, including attaining an altitude of 85,068ft and a speed of 2,092mph.

⋏ One of two Strategic Air Command SR-71As to shatter six existing world altitude and speed records on 27 July 1976. (US National Archives at College Park, Maryland, Still Pictures Branch)

⋏ One of two USAF SR-71As in flight over Beale AFB, California. (US National Archives at College Park, Maryland, Still Pictures Branch)

SR-71A in flight above Beale AFB, California in 1976. (US National Archives at College Park, Maryland, Still Pictures Branch)

Another view of one of the two USAF Strategic Air Command SR-71As in flight above Beale AFB, California, in 1976. (US National Archives at College Park, Maryland, Still Pictures Branch)

▲ A USAF Strategic Air Command SR-71A slated to shatter six existing world altitude and speed records on 27 July 1976 on landing approach to Beale AFB, California, in 1976. (US National Archives at College Park, Maryland, Still Pictures Branch)

▲ Another view of the USAF Strategic Air Command SR-71A on landing approach to Beale AFB, California, in 1976. (US National Archives at College Park, Maryland, Still Pictures Branch)

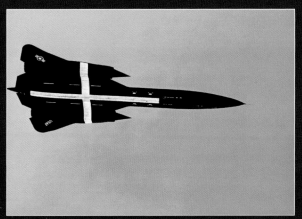

▲ An in-flight underside view of one of three SR-71s that established new world speed and altitude records on 27–28 July 1976. Note the special cross markings on the underside of the aircraft that were used as visual tracking aids to monitor the aircraft at the time of the world record flights. (US National Archives at College Park, Maryland, Still Pictures Branch)

▲ An in-flight view of one of three SR-71s that established new world speed and altitude records on 27–28 July 1976. (US National Archives at College Park, Maryland, Still Pictures Branch)

One of the USAF Strategic Air Command SR-71As in flight over California in 1976. (US National Archives at College Park, Maryland, Still Pictures Branch)

▲ Another view of the USAF Global Shield 79,
1st Strategic Reconnaissance Squadron SR-71A in flight
above Beale AFB, California, in July 1979. (US National
Archives at College Park, Maryland, Still Pictures Branch)

▶ A USAF SR-71A takes off in 1979. (US National
Archives at College Park, Maryland, Still Pictures Branch)

◀ Another view of one of the USAF Strategic Air
Command SR-71As, slated to beat six world altitude and
speed records on 27 July 1976, in flight over California in
1976. (US National Archives at College Park, Maryland,
Still Pictures Branch)

⋏ Another view of the USAF Global Shield 79, 1st Strategic Reconnaissance Squadron SR-71A in flight above Beale AFB, California, in July 1979. (US National Archives at College Park, Maryland, Still Pictures Branch)

⋏ A USAF SR-71A Blackbird on static display at an air show at Beale AFB on 1 August 1981. (US National Archives at College Park, Maryland, Still Pictures Branch)

◂◂ An underside view of the USAF Global Shield 79, 1st Strategic Reconnaissance Squadron SR-71A in flight above Beale AFB, California, in July 1979. (US National Archives at College Park, Maryland, Still Pictures Branch)

◄ A USAF 9th Strategic Reconnaissance Wing SR-71A Blackbird prepares for aerial refueling from a KC-10 Extender during a flight test on 2 August 1981. (US National Archives at College Park, Maryland, Still Pictures Branch)

◄◄ A USAF SR-71A Blackbird in flight on 1 November 1981. (US National Archives at College Park, Maryland, Still Pictures Branch)

⌃ A USAF Blackbird on landing approach on 1 November 1981. (US National Archives at College Park, Maryland, Still Pictures Branch)

⌃ A USAF 9th SRW SR-71A Blackbird takes off from Beale AFB on 2 August 1981 on an aerial refueling feasibility flight test with a KC-10 Extender. (US National Archives at College Park, Maryland, Still Pictures Branch)

⌃⌃ SR-71 taxies back to its hangar at Beale AFB following the successful completion of aerial refueling feasibility flight testing with a KC-10 Extender. (US National Archives at College Park, Maryland, Still Pictures Branch)

⌃ An SR-71B Blackbird in flight during its 1,000th mission on 13 January 1982. (NARA)

⌃ Underside view of SR-71B Blackbird in flight. (US National Archives at College Park, Maryland, Still Pictures Branch)

⌃ A USAF 9th Strategic Reconnaissance Wing SR-71A in flight on 1 February 1982. (US National Archives at College Park, Maryland, Still Pictures Branch)

⌃ The SR-71B Blackbird crew exits their aircraft following the successful completion of its 1,000th mission on 13 January 1982. (US National Archives at College Park, Maryland, Still Pictures Branch)

A USAF SR-71A in flight on 23 April 1985. (US National Archives at College Park, Maryland, Still Pictures Branch)

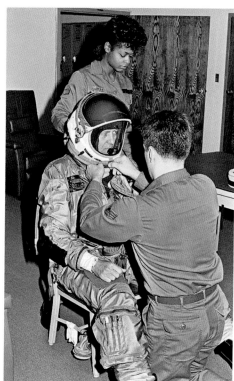

◄◄ Ground crews assist a 9th SRW Blackbird crew as they exit their aircraft following successful aerial refueling feasibility flight testing with a KC-10 Extender on 2 August 1981. (US National Archives at College Park, Maryland, Still Pictures Branch)

◄ Strategic Air Command Commander-in-Chief General Larry D. Welch is prepped by ground crews for a flight in an SR-71 Blackbird on 15 January 1986. (US National Archives at College Park, Maryland, Still Pictures Branch)

❯ A USAF SR-71A Blackbird approaches a tanker aircraft for aerial refueling on 1 January 1988. (US National Archives at College Park, Maryland, Still Pictures Branch)

❯ A Blackbird aircrew, dressed in their high-altitude flight suits, participates in a water survival exercise at Beale AFB, California, on 1 January 1995. (US National Archives at College Park, Maryland, Still Pictures Branch)

➤ A USAF SR-71A in flight on 1 June 1988. (US National Archives at College Park, Maryland, Still Pictures Branch)

∀ A USAF SR-71A on static display at Air Fete 1988 NATO aircraft display, held by the 513th Airborne Command and Control Wing. (US National Archives at College Park, Maryland, Still Pictures Branch)

<< A USAF SR-71A receives maintenance servicing from a ground crewman at sunset. (NARA)

< A USAF SR-71A receives signal from a ground crewman to proceed with take-off preparations. (US National Archives at College Park, Maryland, Still Pictures Branch)

◄ A USAF SR-71A in flight on 1 June 1988. (US National Archives at College Park, Maryland, Still Pictures Branch)

▼ Frontal view of a parked USAF SR-71A receiving service in its hangar at Beale AFB, California. on 1 June 1988. (US National Archives at College Park, Maryland, Still Pictures Branch)

▼ A USAF SR-71B after sundown at Beale AFB, California, on 1 June 1988. (US National Archives at College Park, Maryland, Still Pictures Branch)

⌃ Lieutenant Colonel William R. Dyckman (left) and Lieutenant Colonel Thomas E. Bergam exit their SR-71A at Beale AFB, after flying their last operational mission in their aircraft on 26 January 1990. (US National Archives at College Park, Maryland, Still Pictures Branch)

⌃ Key personnel in the contemporary USAF Blackbird programme pose for a publicity photo in front of the SR-71: (from left to right) an unidentified Lockheed Aircraft Corp. representative, Gen. John T. Chain, Lt Col Thomas E. Bergam, Lt Col William R. Dyckman, Col James S. Savarda, Lt Gen. Richard A. Burpee, Brig. Gen. Kenneth F. Keller and Lt Col Smith. (US National Archives at College Park, Maryland, Still Pictures Branch)

◂◂ A USAF SR-71A in flight on 1 February 1990. (US National Archives at College Park, Maryland, Still Pictures Branch)

◀◀ Pilot Major Terry B. Pappas and Major John D. Manzi exit their 9th SRW SR-71A following the aircraft's arrival at March AFB, California, for the Blackbird's retirement ceremony on 28 February 1990. Note the U-2 in the background. (US National Archives at College Park, Maryland, Still Pictures Branch)

◀ A USAF SR-71A Blackbird arrives at its position of honour at its retirement ceremony at March Field Museum on 1 March 1990. (US National Archives at College Park, Maryland, Still Pictures Branch)

◀ Aerial view of the flight line at the retirement ceremony of the SR-71 Blackbird on 1 March 1990. Note the 22nd Air Refueling Wing KC-135 and KC-10 tankers. (US National Archives at College Park, Maryland, Still Pictures Branch)

Rising tensions in the Middle East and the growing threat North Korea posed to world security during the early 1990s prompted members of the United States Congress to reassess the status of the Blackbirds. Consequently, the US Congress decided that the SR-71's still-advanced intelligence gathering and operational performance capabilities were simply irreplaceable. Therefore, an additional $100 million was allocated to the budget for intelligence-gathering missions of three unretired Blackbirds in 1993. The budgetary allocation, however, was significantly reduced, but Lockheed Skunk Works made the retired Blackbirds operational once again below the adjusted budget allocation. Veteran commanders and aircrews of the Blackbird programme were put in charge of managing and commanding the Blackbird reactivation programme.

The three reactivated Blackbirds, crewed by active USAF pilots and RSOs, were operated by the 9th Reconnaissance Wing based at Beale AFB, California. Efforts were made to outfit the reactivated Blackbirds with a real-time data-link system capable of relaying the aircrafts' advanced radar PHOTINT to ground bases. The reactivated Blackbird missions were launched from Edwards AFB, California. With growing support for the replacement of the Blackbirds with advanced unmanned aerial vehicles (UAVs) or drones within the USAF and aerospace companies, the USAF declared in 1996 that no reactivated Blackbird mission funding had been approved. Therefore, the reactivation programme came to a screeching halt. Although Congress reauthorised reactivated Blackbird mission funding, the Clinton administration vetoed the bill that would have appropriated the required mission funding in October 1997. Despite further deliberations, the USAF permanently retired the Blackbird in 1998.

Did You Know?

In 1998, the USAF permanently retired the Blackbird due to growing support within the USAF and aerospace companies for the aircraft's eventual replacement – the advanced Unmanned Aerial Vehicle (UAV) or drone.

On 15 February 1990, SR-71A (61-7980/NASA 844) landed at NASA Dryden Flight Research Center (DFRC), Edwards, California, for use in NASA Blackbird flight research programmes. Shortly thereafter, on 19 March 1990, SR-71A (61-7971/NASA 832) touched down at NASA DFRC to also serve as a member of NASA's Blackbird flight research fleet. On 25 July 1991, SR-71B (61-7956/NASA 831) landed at NASA DFRC to participate in NASA flight research projects.

The first NASA Blackbird flight research project involved the development and flight-testing of a laser air data collection system. Through the use of this system, flight data was collected via a laser light.

The new technology also yielded important atmospheric particulate data at extremely high altitudes. In March 1993, the NASA SR-71s were outfitted with specially designed science cameras used in airborne astronomy experiments. Scientists at the University of California, Los Angeles (UCLA), also benefited from NASA Blackbird flight research, as one of the NASA aircraft was used in a UCLA experiment designed to determine the effectiveness of charged chlorine atoms intended for utilisation in the protection and regeneration of the ozone layer. The new camera technology developed for use in the NASA Blackbird programme was also intended for use in earth science studies,

The first SR-71 provided to NASA by the USAF lands, with drag chute deployed, at Dryden Flight Research Center in 1990. (NASA DFRC)

Did You Know?

During the 1990s, NASA Blackbirds were used in sonic boom mitigation flight research studies aimed at quieting the 'boom' and reducing undesirable effects experienced on the ground when jet aircraft break the sound barrier.

A NASA SR-71A and NASA F-16XL in flight on a sonic boom mitigation flight research mission during the early to mid 1990s. (NASA DFRC)

including atmospheric and rocket/volcano plume analysis.

The NASA Blackbirds also participated in iridium satellite communication technology development flight research studies.

Finally, NASA Blackbirds were used in sonic boom mitigation flight research studies. NASA also utilised an F-16XL flight research aircraft to fly behind the NASA SR-71A to probe pressure and atmospheric

A NASA SR-71B and NASA F/A-18 chase aircraft on a high-speed/high-altitude flight research mission on 28 January 1997. (NASA Dryden Flight Research Center, Jim Ross)

A NASA SR-71B takes off on a flight research mission in 1992. Note the 'shock diamonds' appearing in the engine exhausts. (NASA DFRC)

conditions within the near-field shockwave. The important data collected from the Blackbird sonic boom mitigation flight research studies will undoubtedly benefit future aircraft designers and manufacturers of supersonic or hypersonic transport aircraft.

On 31 October 1997, the NASA Blackbird flight research programme commenced a research project that would later achieve yet another unprecedented first for the remarkable aircraft. The research project, which became known as the Linear Aerospike SR-71 Experiment (LASRE), called for one of the NASA Blackbirds to be utilised in the flight-testing of the largest test article hauled by the Blackbird to date; the external loads that were absorbed by the aircraft rivalled those borne by the aircraft during Project Tagboard (1964–66) and the M-21/D-21 reconnaissance drone programme. The initial LASRE flight research mission was flown by Blackbird 64-17980 (NASA 844) and took one hour fifty minutes to complete. During the mission, the aircraft attained a top speed of Mach 1.2 and an altitude of 33,000ft.

Then, on 4 March 1998, the NASA LASRE Blackbird successfully performed the first airborne cold-flow

▼ A NASA SR-71A fires up its Dual Max Afterburner Engines in 1998. (NASA DFRC, Tony Landis)

Did You Know?

On 4 March 1998, the NASA LASRE Blackbird successfully performed the first airborne cold-flow test of the Boeing-Rocketdyne 12-S linear aerospike engine, attaining a top speed of Mach 1.2 and an altitude of 33,000ft while transporting one of the largest test articles (payloads) ever carried by the aircraft during the entire Blackbird programme.

▲ The linear aerospike engine is mounted on the NASA LASRE flight research aircraft in a hangar at the NASA DFRC in August 1997. (NASA DFRC, Tony Landis)

test of the Boeing-Rocketdyne 12-S linear aerospike engine. Although the initial flight-test results were encouraging, several cryogenic fuel leaks were detected. As a result, even though the advanced engine was successfully ground-fired twice for three-second durations, NASA decided further Blackbird flight-testing of the linear aerospike engine, and its extremely volatile fuel, would be too risky. Consequently, NASA terminated the LASRE programme in November 1998.

◀ NASA SR-71 pilots and crew (from left to right: Smith, Meyer, Bohn-Meyer, Ishmael) pose for a publicity photo at the NASA DFRC on 1 November 1991. (NASA)

The NASA Blackbirds made their last appearance at the Edwards AFB open house held on 9 and 10 October 1999. Following this event, they were put in 'flyable storage'; NASA hoped that they would later once again be called upon to perform critical 'access to space' flight research missions. These missions, however, would be dependent upon securing funding from ever-shrinking NASA budgets.

Did You Know?

Following the 9–10 October 1999 Edwards AFB open house, NASA's blackbird fleet was retired.

SURVIVING SR-71S AND THEIR DISPOSITIONS

A total of thirty-two Blackbirds were produced, with twelve being lost in crashes (from 1966 to 1972) and one pilot casualty. A listing of surviving Blackbirds and their dispositions is as follows:

1. SR-71A (61-7951): Pima Air & Space Museum, Tucson, Arizona (once served NASA as YF-12A 60-6934).

2. SR-71A (61-7955): Air Force Flight Test Center Museum, Edwards AFB, California.

3. SR-71B (61-7956): Air Zoo, Kalamazoo, Michigan.

4. SR-71A (61-7958): Museum of Aviation, Robins AFB, Warner Robins, Georgia.

5. SR-71A (61-7959): Air Force Armament Museum, Eglin AFB, Florida.

6. SR-71A (61-7960): Castle Air Museum (ex-Castle AFB, Atwater, California).

7. SR-71A (61-7961): Kansas Cosmosphere and Space Center, Hutchinson, Kansas.

▲ A surviving SR-71A at the Pima Air & Space Museum, Tucson, Arizona, in 1999. (Beta75)

8. SR-71A (61-7962): American Air Museum in Britain, Imperial War Museum Duxford, Cambridgeshire, England.

9. SR-71A (61-7963): Beale AFB, Marysville, California.

10. SR-71A (61-7964): Strategic Air Command & Aerospace Museum, Ashland, Nebraska.

11. SR-71A (61-7967): Barksdale AFB, Bossier City, Louisiana.

12. SR-71A (61-7968): Science Museum of Virginia, Richmond, Virginia.

13. SR-71A (61-7971): Evergreen Aviation Museum, McMinnville, Oregon.

14. SR-71A (61-7972): Smithsonian Institution Steven F. Udvar-Hazy Center, Washington, Dulles International Airport, Chantilly, Virginia.

15. SR-71A (61-7973): Blackbird Airpark, Air Force Plant 42, Palmdale, California.

16. SR-71A (61-7975): March Field Air Museum, March Air Reserve Base (ex-March AFB), Riverside, California.

17. SR-71A (61-7976): National Museum of the United States Air Force, Wright-Patterson AFB, close to Dayton, Ohio.

18. SR-71A (61-7979): Lackland AFB, San Antonio, Texas.

19. SR-71A (61-7980): Armstrong Flight Research Center, Edwards AFB, California.

20. SR-71C (61-7981): Hill Aerospace Museum, Hill AFB, Ogden, Utah (ex-YF-12A 60-6934).

NOTES

1. RG 263-a1-27-box-8-94-1, Summer 1982: 8-94-1: 'Development of the Lockheed SR-71 Blackbird', by Clarence L. Johnson, pp. 3–4, US National Archives at College Park, Maryland, Still Pictures Branch, OPA, https://research.archives.gov/id/7283113.
2. Ibid, p. 4.
3. Ibid, p. 6.
4. Ibid.
5. Ibid, p. 7.
6. Ibid, p. 9.
7. Ibid.
8. Ibid, pp. 10–11.
9. Graham, Richard H., *SR-71 Revealed: The Inside Story* (St Paul, Minnesota: MBI Publishing Company, 1996).

➤ A USAF SR-71A on landing approach at Barksdale AFB, Louisiana, in December 1974. (US National Archives at College Park, Maryland, Still Pictures Branch)

▲ A USAF 9th Strategic Reconnaissance Wing SR-71A Blackbird on one of its last operational missions on 1 January 1990. (US National Archives at College Park, Maryland, Still Pictures Branch)